Grade K

Weekly and Unit
Assessments

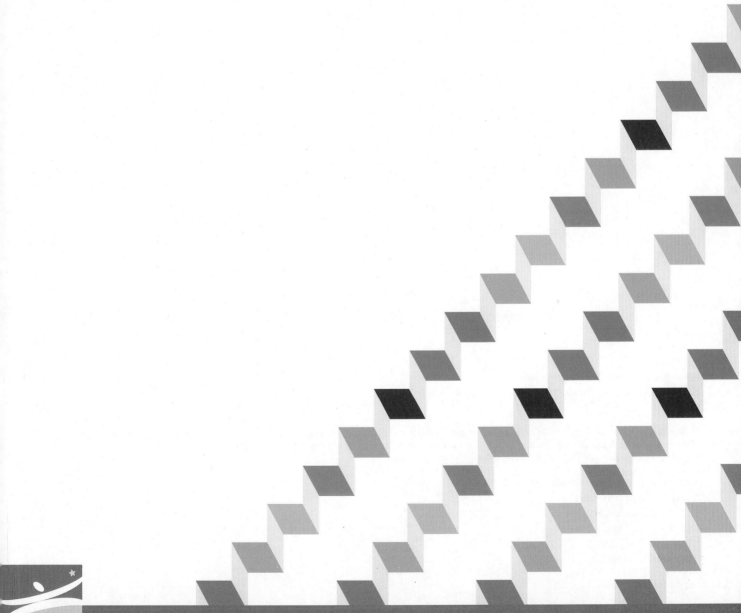

Benchmark EDUCATION

BENCHMARK EDUCATION COMPANY

Benchmark Education Company
145 Huguenot Street • New Rochelle, NY 10801

Senior Project Editors: Sherine Gilmour
Assistant Editor: Nicholas DeLibero
Creative Director: Laurie Berger
Designer: Sophia Oliboni
Director of Photography: Doug Schneider
Photo Assistant: Jackie Friedman

Illustrations: Norm Grock

Printed in Guangzhou, China. 4401/0319/CA21900193
ISBN: 978-1-5125-5194-5

Weekly and Unit Assessments

Table of Contents

Overview

The *Benchmark Advance* literacy program has ten units per grade in Grades K–6. Each three-week unit focuses on a Unit Concept, such as "Technology and Society" or "Point of View," a grade-appropriate topic, and an "essential question." Each unit provides reading selections related to the topic and the essential question. Most units focus on informational or literary genres, although some units offer both. Instruction in each unit focuses on reading comprehension and building language, word study, and writing.

This book provides a set of Weekly and Unit Assessments designed to assess children's grasp of reading and foundational skills taught in each unit. Both the instructional elements and the assessments in each unit are aligned to the Common Core State Standards for each grade level. Descriptions of the Weekly and Unit Assessments are provided in the following sections, along with directions for administering and scoring the assessments, and directions for interpreting scores.

Description of Assessments

Benchmark Advance literacy offers an array of assessments to inform and support the instructional program. In keeping with the Common Core State Standards and the best of current assessment practices, Benchmark assessments use a variety of item types.

Item Types. In Kindergarten, Weekly Assessments are observational. In the Unit Assessments, all questions are selected-response items. Children listen to the questions and select an answer by circling a picture, letter, or word. Grade 1 uses multiple-choice items and writing prompts. In Grades 2–6, the assessments use a wide variety of "nontraditional" and technology-enhanced items.

In Kindergarten Unit Assessments, all reading passages and questions are intended to be read aloud by the teacher. The reading passages do not appear in the student pages, but the title and illustrations do. Children look at the pictures while listening to the passage.

Weekly Assessments

Each unit has two Weekly Assessments based on the instructional content and skills taught in Week 1 and Week 2. To minimize the amount of testing time at this level, the Weekly Assessments are designed as observational checklists. These assessments are intended to provide formative information to help guide instruction as children work through each unit—essentially, to see if children understand what has been taught so far. Information from these assessments can help teachers decide whether to revisit some of the material in the unit or approach it from a different direction in the following week.

For Week 1, the assessment presents a classroom chart that lists the strategies and skills being taught during instruction. These include listening and reading comprehension skills, reading foundational skills such as phonics and high-frequency words. Based on classroom observations during Week 1, the teacher rates each student's progress in the areas listed and records any additional notes or comments on the chart. For Week 2, the teacher does the same with the Week 2 chart.

Unit Assessments

In Kindergarten, the Unit Assessments have two parts: Reading and Reading Foundational Skills.

The Reading section has one passage (intended to be read aloud) and 5 test questions, or items, worth a total of 5 points. The types of passages in the assessment match the kinds of passages taught in the unit, and they reflect the same topics and difficulty levels. The questions assess listening/reading comprehension, cross-text comparisons, and vocabulary skills that have been taught in the unit. Vocabulary skills are tested with words in context from the passages.

The Reading Foundational Skills part of the test has 5 items testing phonics, syllabication, high-frequency words, and the like.

How to Administer the Assessments

The Week 1 Assessment is based on the skills taught in the first week and is intended to be used during and at the end of Week 1.

The Week 2 Assessment is based on the skills taught in the second week and is intended to be used during and at the end of Week 2.

The Unit Assessment is based on the skills taught in Weeks 1–3 and is intended to be administered at the end of the unit in Week 3.

Teachers may choose not to use all three assessments in a unit. If children all seem to do well on Week 1 in a given unit, for example, the teacher may decide to omit the Week 2 Assessment and administer the Unit Assessment at the end of the unit.

For Kindergarten, the Week 1 and Week 2 Assessments are intended to be used during and after regular classroom activities, wherever and whenever appropriate. They are designed as quick observational checks and should not require a lot of additional time. For the Unit Assessments, the chart below shows the estimated time for administration.

Estimated Times for Administration (in Minutes)		
Assessment	Reading	Reading Foundational Skills
Unit Assessment	10	5

The Unit Assessment may be administered in one or two sittings. For example, the Reading section could be administered in one sitting and the Reading Foundational Skills section in a second sitting.

These time allowances are for planning purposes only. These assessments are not intended to be timed; children should be allowed more time if needed.

Directions for Using a Weekly Assessment

1. Make a copy of the assessment chart for your classroom.

2. Write children's names in the first column.

3. As part of the instructional planning for the week, identify times when children will be engaged in activities involving the skills listed on the chart. For example, if one skill is "retell key details," then identify times when children will be engaged in small-group reading activities. You may observe children's abilities to "retell key details" during these activities.

4. There are various ways to conduct an assessment of this kind. You may choose five children to observe each day, or you may choose a few skills to look for among all the children. With whatever approach you take, try to observe children at different times and in different settings.

5. Record your observations on the chart by rating children's skills (1, 2, or 3) and writing comments to clarify things you observe. For example, you may note that a student pronounces words with the "Initial p" sound sometimes and give that student a "2" rating for "Initial p." But then you may notice that the student can pronounce "Initial p" words but does not recognize them in print. This observation may be important in how you approach the student's instruction and should be recorded on the chart.

6. One more note: You should not feel compelled to fill in every box on the chart for every student every week. This kind of assessment is intended to be an easy, natural way to record what you observe in the course of a day, and that level of information can be very helpful in your planning. It may also be useful for reporting to parents, other teachers, and administrators, if required. Keep a record of observations to whatever level is helpful for these purposes.

Directions for Administering a Unit Assessment

1. Make a copy of the assessment for each student. The Unit Assessment is recommended for administration to individuals, one-on-one, or in small groups of 4–5 children.

2. Unless the children are able to write their own names, write the student's name and the date at the top of the first page.

3. Read the directions for the teacher at the top of the first page. Tell children you will be reading a passage aloud and then asking some questions. Then read the passage and the questions. Allow time for children to answer each question before proceeding to the next one.

   As noted earlier: In Kindergarten Unit Assessments, all passages and questions are intended to be read aloud by the teacher. The passages do not appear in the student pages, but the title and illustrations do. Children look at the pictures while listening to the passage.

4. For multiple-choice questions, tell children to choose the best answer to each question and circle the answer. (The answer may be a picture, a letter, or a word.) If necessary in early units, show children how to draw a circle.

5. Monitor children as they work on the assessment to make sure they are following directions and know what to do.

6. When children have finished, collect the assessments.

How to Use Information from the Weekly Assessments

1. The Week 1 and 2 Assessments are observational assessments intended to provide formative information. Children may demonstrate certain skills all the time ("Always") or "Sometimes"; or they may not demonstrate the skills at all ("Not Yet"). Consider the Weekly Assessment as a guide to help you determine what each student has learned so far and what the student may need more time and more help to develop.

2. Look for progress from each student. A student who has a lot of "Not Yet" ratings in Week 1, for example, but only half as many in Week 2 has made significant progress. If you notice that a student does not seem to be making progress in certain areas, that may indicate a need for further observation or individualized help.

3. Look for trends across the classroom. For example, if a large number of children cannot demonstrate a particular skill, such as "Making Inferences" or "Using Text Features," then you can use that information to help plan instruction for the following week or the next unit.

How to Score the Unit Assessments

1. Make a copy of the Unit Assessment Scoring Chart for each student (or you may choose to mark all scores on the test itself).

2. Refer to the Answer Key for the Unit Assessment. It gives the correct response for each question.

3. For each question, compare the student's answer with the answer key. If the student's answer is correct, put a check mark (✔) beside the item number. If it is incorrect (or blank), cross out the item number with an X.

4. To find the total test score for Reading and Reading Foundational Skills, add the number of correct responses (check marks). In the Unit Assessment, the total score = number correct/10.

Using the Unit Assessment Results

On a Unit Assessment, the student's score will help determine how well the student grasped the standards and skills taught in the unit. You may look at a student's score as a number correct or a percent (number correct ÷ total number of points).

To find a percent score based on the number correct, refer to the table below. A score of 90–100 percent correct is excellent; 80–89 percent is good; 70–79 percent is proficient. Anything below 70 percent would merit further analysis, which could indicate a need for additional instruction in the following week or in following units. A score below 50 percent could indicate a need for reteaching before the student moves to the next week or unit.

Webb's Depth of Knowledge

During standardized reading assessments, students are required to answer different levels of text-dependent comprehension questions. These questions require application of different levels of Webb's Depth of Knowledge—recall, skill/concept, strategic, and extended thinking. Keep these question levels in mind to focus on comprehension development. The questions in each Assessment provide opportunities for students to rehearse strategies for answering each type of question. Please note that a few questions do not target a specific literary claim.

Level of Complexity	Question Type
1	**Recall/Reproduction** Recall a fact, information, or procedure; process information on a low level
2	**Skill/Concept** Use information or conceptual knowledge, two or more steps
3	**Strategic Thinking** Requires reasoning, developing a plan or a sequence of steps, more than one reasonable approach
4	**Extended Thinking** Requires connections and extensions, high cognitive demands and complex reasoning

Number Correct (Points)	Total Points: 5	Total Points: 10
1	20	10
2	40	20
3	60	30
4	80	40
5	100	50
6		60
7		70
8		80
9		90
10		100

For a more detailed analysis of a student's score, refer to the Answer Key. For each item, the Answer Key indicates the tested standard or skill. Most standards and skills are tested by more than one item. Identifying which items the student answered incorrectly can help determine whether more focused instruction on particular standards or skills is needed. For example, a student may answer questions about Key Details correctly but have trouble with questions that require Making Inferences. Instruction for this student in the next week or following unit may require more focus on this strategy.

Reviewing a student's assessment with the student may also be helpful. It can provide an opportunity for children to see which questions they answered incorrectly and why their answers were incorrect. This kind of review will help them be more successful next time.

To monitor a student's scores across all units, use the Classroom Unit Assessment Scoring Chart. Record the student's score on each unit assessment to help determine whether the student's test scores are improving or staying about the same as he or she moves through the units. This kind of review may also indicate that certain children need additional help in the literary units, or in the informational units, and this kind of information can help guide instruction.

Unit _____ Assessment Scoring Chart   Date _____

Student's Name _____   Teacher Name _____

Item Number	Number Correct (✓'s)	Total Score
Item		
Number	Number	
Correct (□'s)		
Total Score		
1		
2		
3		
4		
5		
Reading		___/5 = ___%
6		
7		
8		
9		
10		
Reading Foundational Skills		___/5 = ___%
Total		___/10 = ___%

Classroom Unit Assessment Scoring Chart

Teacher Name _____   Class _____

Directions: Record each student's Total Test score and Writing score on the Unit Assessment for each unit.

Student Name	Unit 1	Unit 2	Unit 3	Unit 4	Unit 5	Unit 6	Unit 7	Unit 8	Unit 9	Unit 10

Reading Skills and Strategy Assessment

Teacher's Name _____ Class _____ Date _____

Directions: Based on classroom observations during Week 1, rate each student's progress in the areas listed below by marking 1, 2, or 3 in the box below each statement. 1=Not Yet; 2=Sometimes; 3=Always. Record any additional notes or comments in the Comments column or at the bottom of the page.

Student Name	Retell Key Events	Identify Characters in a Story	Alphabet Review	Comments/Notes

Foundational Skills Assessment

Teacher's Name _____ Class _____ Date _____

Alphabet Review

Directions: To assess or verify the student's reading foundational skills, ask the student to name the letters in each row. Circle each letter the child names correctly.

d	H	p	C	x
k	E	i	m	s
w	T	L	A	f
b	U	o	N	g
J	q	V	R	y	Z

Reading Skills and Strategy Assessment

Teacher's Name _____ Class _____ Date _____

Directions: Based on classroom observations during Week 2, rate each student's progress in the areas listed below by marking 1, 2, or 3 in the box below each statement. 1=Not Yet; 2=Sometimes; 3=Always. Record any additional notes or comments in the Comments column or at the bottom of the page.

Student Name	Retell Key Events	Identify Parts of a Book	Identify Author's Reasons	Use Text Features: Glossary, Captions, Sidebar	Connect Illustrations and Text	Initial/ Final *m*	Comments/Notes

Foundational Skills Assessment

Teacher's Name _____ Class _____ Date _____

Initial/Final *m*
High-Frequency Words

Directions: To assess or verify the student's reading foundational skills:

1. Read the words in the first row. Ask the student to point to the words that begin with m. Circle each word the child identifies correctly.

2. Read the words in the second row. Ask the student to point to the words that end with m. Circle each word the child identifies correctly.

3. Point to the last row. Ask the student to read the word I. Circle the word I if the student the word I.

mat	cat	man	pan
jam	jet	gull	gum
I	like		

Teacher Administration:
Read the passage aloud as children look at the illustrations.
Then read each question along with the answer choices. Have
children circle the correct answer to each question.

Nap Time

"It's time to rest," said Mrs. James.

"I don't need a rest," said George. "I never take a nap at home. I'm five!"

"You may look at a book. You must lie quietly on your mat," said Mrs. James. "Some children are very tired." She pointed to Sari. George's friend was sound asleep on the mat nearby.

George looked at his book. He yawned. He looked at a few more pages. He stretched. His eyes felt heavy. "No way I'm taking a nap," he said to himself.

"George," called Mrs. James. She shook him gently. "It's time for science," she said. "You need to wake up now."

George yawned and stretched again. Now he felt full of energy. Maybe naps weren't a bad thing after all.

Reading Questions

> **Say**: Now I'm going to read some questions. Follow along as I read.

1. Find the picture of the apple. Look at the pictures in the row. Which picture shows George at the beginning of the story? Draw a circle around the picture that shows George at the beginning of the story.

continued ➡

2. Find the picture of the bell. Look at the pictures in the row. Who tells George it is nap time? Draw a circle around the picture.

3. Find the picture of the truck. Look at the pictures in the row. Who is this story all about? Is it about Mrs. James . . . George . . . or Sari? Circle the picture.

4. Find the picture of the pencil. Look at the pictures in the row. What does the teacher want George to do next: read a book . . . take a nap . . . or study science? Circle the picture.

5. Find the picture of the boot. Look at the pictures in the row. What does Sari do when George is reading? Does she look at a plant . . . take a nap . . . or read a book? Circle your answer.

Reading Foundational Skills Questions

Say: Now look at the next page. I am going to ask some more questions.

6. Find the picture of the spoon. Look at the letters in the row. Find the letter <u>h</u> . . . <u>h</u>. Draw a circle around the answer.

7. Find the picture of the banana. Look at the words in the row. Listen as I read the words: map . . . tap . . . sap. Circle the word that begins with <u>m</u>: <u>map</u> . . . <u>tap</u> . . . <u>sap</u>.

8. Find the picture of the chair. Look at the words in the row. Listen as I read the words: rip . . . rib . . . rim. Circle the word that ends with <u>m</u>: <u>rip</u> . . . <u>rib</u> . . . <u>rim</u>.

9. Find the picture of the mitten. Look at the words in the row. Listen as I read the words: sit . . . sat . . . set. Circle the word that has the <u>a</u> sound, as in am: <u>sit</u> . . . <u>sat</u> . . . <u>set</u>.

10. Find the picture of the umbrella. Look at the words in the row. Listen: I like to run. Find the word <u>like</u> . . . <u>like</u>. Circle your answer.

Nap Time

1.

2.

3.

4.

5.

6.

b   p   h

7.

map   tap   sap

8.

rip   rib   rim

9.

sit   sat   set

10.

I   like   run

STOP!

Reading Skills and Strategy Assessment

Teacher's Name _____ Class _____ Date _____

Directions: Based on classroom observations during Week 1, rate each student's progress in the areas listed below by marking 1, 2, or 3 in the box below each statement. 1=Not Yet; 2=Sometimes; 3=Always. Record any additional notes or comments in the Comments column or at the bottom of the page.

Student Name	Retell Key Details	Identify Genre: Fantasy	Identify Story Characters	Make Inferences	Identify Story Events	Vocabulary: Shades of Meanings	Initial	High-Frequency Words	Comments/Notes

Foundational Skills Assessment

Teacher's Name _____ Class _____ Date _____

Initial *s*
High-Frequency Words

Directions: To assess or verify the student's reading foundational skills:

1. Read the words in the first row. Ask the student to point to the words that begin with *s*.

2. Point to the second row. Ask the student to read the words. Circle each word the student identifies correctly.

run   sun   sad   mad

We like the   .

Reading Skills and Strategy Assessment

Teacher's Name _____ Class _____ Date _____

Directions: Based on classroom observations during Week 2, rate each student's progress in the areas listed below by marking 1, 2, or 3 in the box below each statement. 1=Not Yet; 2=Sometimes; 3=Always. Record any additional notes or comments in the Comments column or at the bottom of the page.

Student Name	Retell Key Details	Identify Story Characters	Make Inferences	Identify Story Events	Text Evidence: Fantasy	Vocabulary: Shades of Meaning	Initial/ Final *t*	High- Frequency Words	Comments/Notes

Foundational Skills Assessment

Teacher's Name _____ Class _____ Date _____

Initial/Final *t*
High-Frequency Words

Directions: To assess or verify the student's reading foundational skills:

1. Read the words in the first row. Ask the student to point to the words that begin with *t*.

2. Read the words in the second row. Ask the student to point to the words that end with *t*.

3. Point to the last row. Ask the student to read the words. Circle each word the student identifies correctly.

nip	tip	tub	rub
pit	pin	at	am
see	go	the	

Teacher Administration:
Read the passage aloud as children look at the illustrations.
Then read each question along with the answer choices. Have
children circle the correct answer to each question.

Special in Their Own Way

Camel, Elephant, and Zebra watched people walk by. "People walk on just two legs," said Camel. "They look funny, don't they?"

"You look pretty funny yourself," said Elephant. "What's that on your back?"

"That's my hump," said Camel. "It helps me go without food for many days."

Then Camel said, "Elephant, you look funny. You have such a long nose!"

"My nose is very useful," said Elephant. "It helps me when I drink or take a bath."

Then Elephant said, "Zebra, you look funny. You are covered with stripes."

Zebra said, "My stripes help me hide. They keep me safe from Lion."

"My friends," said Elephant, "we are all different. And we are each special in our own way."

"Agreed," said Camel. "But I still don't understand why people walk on just two legs. They are funny, aren't they?"

continued →

Reading Questions

> **Say**: Now I'm going to read some questions. Follow along as
> I read.

1. Find the picture of the apple. Look at the pictures in the row. What does Camel do at the beginning of the story? Does he walk . . . laugh . . . or eat? Draw a circle around the picture that shows what Camel does at the beginning of the story.

2. Find the picture of the bell. Look at the pictures in the row. Which animal uses his nose to take a bath? Draw a circle around the picture.

3. Find the picture of the truck. Look at the pictures in the row. What animal does Zebra hide from: Lion . . . Tiger . . . or Horse? Circle the picture of the animal Zebra hides from.

4. Find the picture of the pencil. Look at the pictures in the row. How can you tell that this is a make-believe story? Is it because the animals talk . . . the people walk on two legs . . . or the elephant has a trunk? Circle your answer.

5. Find the picture of the boot. Look at the pictures in the row. Elephant and Zebra think that Camel is funny. Which part of him do they think is funny? Circle your answer.

Reading Foundational Skills Questions

Say: Now turn to the next page. I am going to ask some
more questions.

6. Find the picture of the spoon. Look at the words in the row. Find the
word <u>sat</u> . . . <u>sat</u>. Draw a circle around the answer.

7. Find the picture of the banana. Look at the words in the row. Find the
word <u>tap</u> . . . <u>tap</u>. Draw a circle around the answer.

8. Find the picture of the chair. Look at the words in the row. Find the
word <u>an</u> . . . <u>an</u>. Circle your answer.

9. Find the picture of the mitten. Look at the words in the row. Find the
word <u>I</u> . . . <u>I</u>. Circle your answer.

10. Find the picture of the umbrella. Look at the words in the row. Find
the word <u>go</u> . . . <u>go</u>. Circle your answer.

Special in Their Own Way

1.

2.

3.

4.

5.

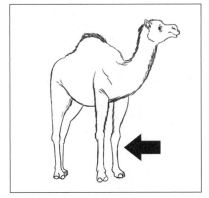  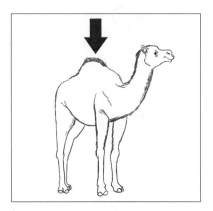

6.

sat   mat   Nat

7.

map   tap   sap

8.

am   at   an

9.

like   I   the

10.

we   go   see

Reading Skills and Strategy Assessment

Teacher's Name _____ Class _____ Date _____

Directions: Based on classroom observations during Week 1, rate each student's progress in the areas listed below by marking 1, 2, or 3 in the box below each statement. 1=Not Yet; 2=Sometimes; 3=Always. Record any additional notes or comments in the Comments column or at the bottom of the page.

Student Name	Retell Key Details	Sequence of Events	Connect Illustrations and Events	Use Text Features: Labels	Identify Author's Reasons	Use Context Clues	Initial/ Medial Short *i*	High- Frequency Words	Comments/ Notes

Foundational Skills Assessment

Teacher's Name _____ Class _____ Date _____

Initial/Medial Short *i*
High-Frequency Words

Directions: To assess or verify the student's reading foundational skills, ask the student to read the words in each row. Circle each word the student reads correctly.

is	it	in
sit	tin	
can	she	

Reading Skills and Strategy Assessment

Teacher's Name _____   Class _____   Date _____

Directions: Based on classroom observations during Week 2, rate each student's progress in the areas listed below by marking 1, 2, or 3 in the box below each statement. 1=Not Yet; 2=Sometimes; 3=Always. Record any additional notes or comments in the Comments column or at the bottom of the page.

Student Name	Retell Key Details	Sequence of Events	Connect Illustrations and Events	Use Text Features: Labels	Identify Author's Reasons	Use Context Clues	Initial *f*	High-Frequency Words	Comments/Notes

Foundational Skills Assessment

Teacher's Name _____ Class _____ Date _____

Initial *f*
High-Frequency Words

Directions: To assess or verify the student's reading foundational skills, ask the student to read the words in each row. Circle each word the student reads correctly.

fit	fan	fat

She is a .

Teacher Administration:
Read the passage aloud as children look at the illustrations. Then read each question along with the answer choices. Have children circle the correct answer to each question.

Venus Flytraps

Plants need sun. They need water. Most green plants get water through their roots. They use sunlight to make food in their green leaves.

Venus flytraps are like other plants in many ways. They need sunlight. They get water through their roots.

Venus flytraps are also unlike most plants in a special way. These plants eat meat! Their leaves look like little jaws with sharp teeth. The leaves can open or snap shut, like your jaws.

The plant leaves are often open. Then an insect comes close. It touches tiny hairs on the edge of a leaf. That makes the leaf snap tight. The insect gets trapped inside. It becomes the plant's next meal.

Reading Questions

Say: Now I'm going to read some questions. Follow along as I read.

1. Find the picture of the apple. Look at the pictures in the row. What does a Venus flytrap eat? Does it eat flies . . . leaves . . . or roots? Draw a circle around the picture that shows what a Venus flytrap eats.

2. Find the picture of the bell. The passage says the leaves of the plant open like your <u>jaws</u>. Look at the pictures in the row. Which picture shows a <u>jaw</u>? Draw a circle around the picture.

continued →

3. Find the picture of the truck. Look at the pictures in the row. Which picture shows the Venus flytrap after it catches food? Circle the picture.

4. Find the picture of the pencil. Look at the pictures in the row. The author says the Venus flytrap is unlike other plants because it needs what: sunshine . . . insects . . . or rain? Circle the picture.

5. Find the picture of the boot. Look at the pictures in the row. Which picture shows the *leaf* label on the correct part of the drawing? Circle your answer.

Reading Foundational Skills Questions

Say: Now look at the next page. I am going to ask some more questions.

6. Find the picture of the spoon. Look at the words in the row. Find the word <u>sit</u> . . . <u>sit</u>. Draw a circle around the answer.

7. Find the picture of the banana. Look at the words in the row. Find the word <u>fan</u> . . . <u>fan</u>. Circle your answer.

8. Find the picture of the chair. Look at the words in the row. Find the word <u>map</u> . . . <u>map</u>. Circle your answer.

9. Find the picture of the mitten. Look at the words in the row. Listen: We have fun. Find the word <u>we</u> . . . <u>we</u>. Circle your answer.

10. Find the picture of the umbrella. Look at the words in the row. Listen: You can run fast. Find the word <u>can</u> . . . <u>can</u>. Circle your answer.

Venus Flytraps

1.

2.

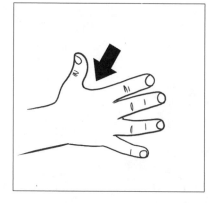 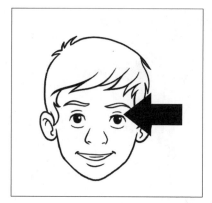 

3.

4.

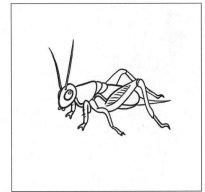

5.

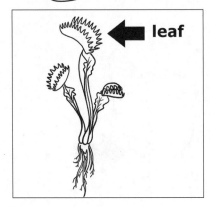

leaf

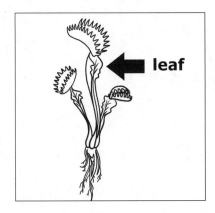

leaf

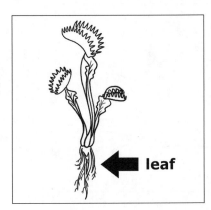

leaf

6.

sat   see   sit

7.

Nan   fan   pan

8.

map   mat   man

9.

the　　　　　**we**　　　　　**see**

10.

like　　　　　**go**　　　　　**can**

Reading Skills and Strategy Assessment

Teacher's Name _____   Class _____   Date _____

Directions: Based on classroom observations during Week 1, rate each student's progress in the areas listed below by marking 1, 2, or 3 in the box below each statement. 1=Not Yet; 2=Sometimes; 3=Always. Record any additional notes or comments in the Comments column or at the bottom of the page.

Student Name	Retell Key Details	Make, Confirm Predictions	Identify Story Events	Vocabulary: Inflections	Vocabulary: Clarify New Meanings	Initial/ Medial Short o High-Frequency Words	Comments/Notes

Foundational Skills Assessment

Teacher's Name _____ Class _____ Date _____

Initial/Medial Short *o*
High-Frequency Words

Directions: To assess or verify the student's reading foundational skills, ask the student to read the words in each row. Circle each word the student reads correctly.

on	Tom	not
	top	pot	
	he	has	

Reading Skills and Strategy Assessment

Teacher's Name _____ Class _____ Date _____

Directions: Based on classroom observations during Week 2, rate each student's progress in the areas listed below by marking 1, 2, or 3 in the box below each statement. 1=Not Yet; 2=Sometimes; 3=Always. Record any additional notes or comments in the Comments column or at the bottom of the page.

Student Name	Retell Key Ideas	Identify Story Elements	Make, Confirm Predictions	Role of Author and Illustrator	Vocabulary: Inflections	Vocabulary: Real-Life Connections	Initial c	High-Frequency Words	Comments/Notes

Foundational Skills Assessment

Teacher's Name _____ Class _____ Date _____

Initial *c*
High-Frequency Words

Directions: To assess or verify the student's reading foundational skills:

1. Read the words in the first row. Ask the student to point to the words that begin with *c*.

2. Point to the second row. Ask the student to read the words. Circle each word the student reads correctly.

cop	pot	rub	cub
The little cat can play.			

Teacher Administration:
Read the passage aloud as children look at the illustrations.
Then read each question along with the answer choices. Have
children circle the correct answer to each question.

The Naughty Puppy

Danny's dog had puppies. "We will give them away," said Danny's mom. They went to the park.

The smallest puppy was all brown. Her brother sat on her.

"Poor little puppy!" said a woman. "I want that one."

Danny said good-bye to the little brown puppy.

The two puppies played. The big puppy bit his brother on the ear. The little spotted puppy cried and cried.

"Poor little puppy!" said a man. "I want that one."

Danny said good-bye to the little spotted puppy.

More people came by. "Is that a nice puppy?" they asked.

"Not always," said Danny. Nobody wanted the naughty puppy.

Finally, a girl came by. "I have wanted a puppy for a long time," said the girl. "Do you have any puppies left?"

continued ➡

Reading Questions

> **Say:** Now I'm going to read some questions. Follow along as
> I read.

1. Find the picture of the apple. Look at the pictures in the row. Which picture shows the puppies at the beginning of the story? Draw a circle around the picture.

2. Find the picture of the bell. Look at the pictures in the row. Which picture shows something a puppy needs? Does it need a hat . . . food . . . or a coat? Draw a circle around the picture.

3. Find the picture of the truck. Look at the pictures in the row. Who takes the little brown puppy: the woman . . . the girl . . . or the man? Draw a circle around the person who takes the little brown puppy.

4. Find the picture of the pencil. Look at the pictures in the row. What will probably happen next? Circle the picture.

5. Find the picture of the boot. Think about the pictures that go with the story. What does the illustrator show in the pictures that the author does not tell you in the story? There were four puppies . . . the boy likes all the puppies . . . or the puppies were in a box? Circle your answer.

Reading Foundational Skills Questions

Say: Now turn to the next page. I am going to ask some more questions.

6. Find the picture of the spoon. Look at the words in the row. Find the word <u>pot</u> . . . <u>pot</u>. Draw a circle around the word.

7. Find the picture of the banana. Look at the words in the row. Find the word <u>cap</u> . . . <u>cap</u>. Draw a circle around the word.

8. Find the picture of the chair. Look at the words in the row. Find the word <u>hat</u> . . . <u>hat</u>. Draw a circle around the word.

9. Find the picture of the mitten. Look at the words in the row. Listen: She can run. Find the word <u>she</u> . . . <u>she</u>. Draw a circle around the word.

10. Find the picture of the umbrella. Look at the words in the row. Listen: He has a cat. Find the word <u>has</u> . . . <u>has</u>. Draw a circle around the word.

The Naughty Puppy

Grade K • Benchmark Advance Weekly and Unit Assessments • © Benchmark Education Company, LLC

1.

2.

3.

Grade K • Benchmark Advance Weekly and Unit Assessments • © Benchmark Education Company, LLC

4.

5.

6.

pot　　　　**pat**　　　　**pit**

7.

tap　　　　**sap**　　　　**cap**

8.

fat　　　　**hat**　　　　**sat**

9.

we   she   see

10.

is   he   has

STOP!

Reading Skills and Strategy Assessment

Teacher's Name _____ Class _____ Date _____

Directions: Based on classroom observations during Week 1, rate each student's progress in the areas listed below by marking 1, 2, or 3 in the box below each statement. 1=Not Yet; 2=Sometimes; 3=Always. Record any additional notes or comments in the Comments column or at the bottom of the page.

Student Name	Retell Key Details	Text Features: Illustrations, Captions	Vocabulary: Identify New Meanings	Vocabulary: Sort Objects Into Categories	Initial/ Final *b*	High- Frequency Words	Comments/Notes

Foundational Skills Assessment

Teacher's Name _____ Class _____ Date _____

Initial/Final *b*
High-Frequency Words

Directions: To assess or verify the student's reading foundational skills:

1. Read the words in the first row. Ask the student to point to the words that begin with *b*.

2. Read the words in the second row. Ask the student to point to the words that end with *b*.

3. Point to the third row. Ask the student to read the words. Circle each word the student reads correctly.

bun	fun	pad	bad
hub	hut	cab	cap
You and I can go.			

Reading Skills and Strategy Assessment

Teacher's Name _____ Class _____ Date _____

Directions: Based on classroom observations during Week 2, rate each student's progress in the areas listed below by marking 1, 2, or 3 in the box below each statement. 1=Not Yet; 2=Sometimes; 3=Always. Record any additional notes or comments in the Comments column or at the bottom of the page.

Student Name	Retell Key Details	Text Features: Illustrations, and Captions	Connect Text and Photos	Identify Author's Reasons	Vocabulary: Opposites	Vocabulary: Identify New Meanings	Initial/ Medial Short *u*	High-Frequency Words	Comments/ Notes

Foundational Skills Assessment

Teacher's Name _____ Class _____ Date _____

Initial/Medial Short *u*
High-Frequency Words

Directions: To assess or verify the student's reading foundational skills, ask the student to read the words in each row. Circle each word the student reads correctly.

us		up
fun	hut	cub
with		big

Teacher Administration:
Read the passage aloud as children look at the illustrations.
Then read each question along with the answer choices. Have
children circle the correct answer to each question.

Working with Wind

Have you ever seen a windmill? The wind makes it work. Many machines use wind. Many toys do, too. Kites float in the wind. A pinwheel turns as wind pushes on it.

Long ago, people did not have electricity. They could not use it to run machines. They used wind power instead. The wind turned the arms on windmills. The arms were connected to a big stone. The stone was used to grind corn or wheat into flour.

Today, people have new machines. They use wind to make electricity. These machines work well in places with lots of wind. You might use this power to run the lights or warm your home.

Reading Questions

> **Say:** Now I'm going to read some questions. Follow along as I read.

1. Find the picture of the apple. Look at the pictures in the row. The passage gives a special meaning for the word <u>arm</u>. Which picture shows this meaning? Circle the picture.

2. Find the picture of the bell. Look at the pictures in the row. Which picture shows a toy that uses wind? Circle the picture of a toy that uses wind.

continued ➤

3. Find the picture of the truck. The passage shows a picture of a pinwheel. What do the arrows show in the pinwheel picture on page 59: how to make a pinwheel . . . how to grind flour . . . or where the wind comes from? Circle the answer.

4. Find the picture of the pencil. Look at the pictures in the row. How did people use windmills long ago? Did they use them to play games . . . to make flour . . . or to make electricity? Circle the picture.

5. Find the picture of the boot. Look at the pictures in the row. According to the author, why did people use the wind long ago? Was it because they liked windmills . . . they did not have electricity . . . or they needed a lamp? Circle your answer.

Reading Foundational Skills Questions

Say: Now look at the next page. I am going to ask some more questions.

6. Find the picture of the spoon. Look at the words in the row. Find the word <u>bat</u> . . . <u>bat</u>. Draw a circle around the word.

7. Find the picture of the banana. Look at the words in the row. Find the word <u>cub</u> . . . <u>cub</u>. Draw a circle around the word.

8. Find the picture of the chair. Look at the words in the row. Find the word <u>ran</u> . . . <u>ran</u>. Draw a circle around the word.

9. Find the picture of the mitten. Look at the words in the row. Listen: He has a big dog. Find the word <u>big</u> . . . <u>big</u>. Draw a circle around the word.

10. Find the picture of the umbrella. Look at the words in the row. Listen: Can you go with me? Find the word <u>you</u> . . . <u>you</u>. Draw a circle around the word.

Working with Wind

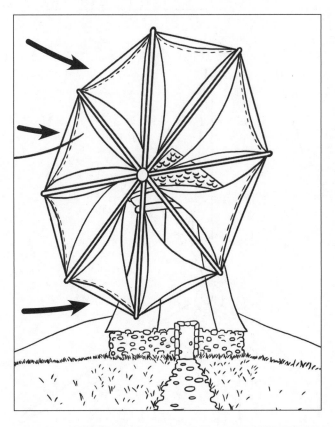

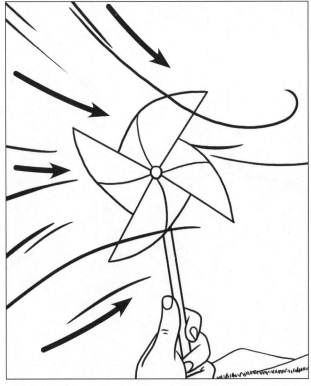

1.

2.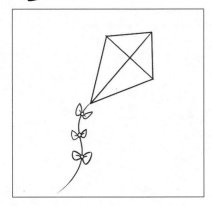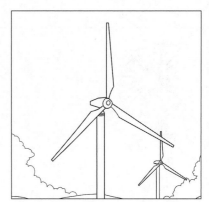

3.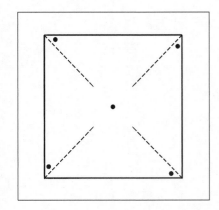

4.

5.

6.

hat   pat   bat

7.

cub   cab   cob

8.

fan   ran   man

9.

with   **little**   **big**

10.

you   **go**   **has**

STOP!

Reading Skills and Strategy Assessment

Teacher's Name _____ Class _____ Date _____

Directions: Based on classroom observations during Week 1, rate each student's progress in the areas listed below by marking 1, 2, or 3 in the box below each statement. 1=Not Yet; 2=Sometimes; 3=Always. Record any additional notes or comments in the Comments column or at the bottom of the page.

Student Name	Retell Key Details	Identify Story Elements	Identify Central Message	Connect Illustrations and Events	Make Inferences About Characters	Vocabulary: Opposites	Vocabulary: Shades of Meaning	Initial/ Medial Short e	Plurals with -s	High-Frequency Words	Comments/ Notes

Foundational Skills Assessment

Teacher's Name _____ Class _____ Date _____

Initial/Medial Short *e*
High-Frequency Words

Directions: To assess or verify the student's reading foundational skills, ask the student to read the words in each row. Circle each word the student reads correctly.

net	men	Ed
fed		bet
for		no

Reading Skills and Strategy Assessment

Teacher's Name _____   Class _____   Date _____

Directions: Based on classroom observations during Week 2, rate each student's progress in the areas listed below by marking 1, 2, or 3 in the box below each statement. 1=Not Yet; 2=Sometimes; 3=Always. Record any additional notes or comments in the Comments column or at the bottom of the page.

Student Name	Retell Key Details	Central Message	Connect Illustrations and Events	Make Inferences About Characters	Vocabulary: Opposites	Vocabulary: Words Ending in -ed	Initial/ Final g	High- Frequency Words	Comments/ Notes

Foundational Skills Assessment

Teacher's Name _____ Class _____ Date _____

Initial/Final *g*
High-Frequency Words

Directions: To assess or verify the student's reading foundational skills, ask the student to read the words in each row. Circle each word the student reads correctly.

hum	gum	cap	gap
rug	rub	tan	tag
I see one bug. It can jump.			

Teacher Administration:
Read the passage aloud as children look at the illustrations.
Then read each question along with the answer choices. Have
children circle the correct answer to each question.

Fox and Stork

One day Fox invited Stork to dinner. He wanted to play a trick on Stork. Fox made some soup. He served it in a flat, wide bowl. He knew that Stork's beak could not get the soup.

"It looks like you are not hungry," said Fox. "I will eat it so it does not go to waste."

Stork went home hungry. She was not happy with Fox. Stork decided to teach Fox a lesson. "Please come for dinner at my house," she said. Fox said yes, of course.

Fox could hardly wait for dinner at Stork's house. He did not eat all day. He planned to eat as much as he could.

Stork had a surprise for Fox. She served soup in a tall, narrow glass.

Fox could not fit his nose into the glass. He just sat there, hungry.

When Fox left, Stork said, "Next time, treat others like you want them to treat you."

continued →

Reading Questions

Say: Now I'm going to read some questions. Follow along as I read.

1. Find the picture of the apple. Look at the pictures in the row. Stork served soup in a <u>narrow</u> glass. Which picture shows the **opposite** of <u>narrow</u>? Circle the picture.

2. Find the picture of the bell. Look at the pictures in the row. What can you tell about Stork from the story? Is she a good friend to Fox . . . wiser than Fox . . . or meaner than Fox? Circle the answer.

3. Find the picture of the truck. Look at the pictures in the row. Which picture shows the beginning of the story? Circle the answer.

4. Find the picture of the pencil. Look at the pictures in the row. Which picture shows what happens at Stork's house? Circle the picture.

5. Find the picture of the boot. Look at the pictures in the row. Which sentence tells the lesson of the story? "He wanted to play a trick on Stork." "I will eat it so it does not go to waste." OR "Next time, treat others like you want them to treat you." Circle the picture that shows the lesson in the story.

Reading Foundational Skills Questions

> **Say:** Now turn to the next page. I am going to ask some
> more questions.

6. Find the picture of the spoon. Look at the words in the row. Find the
word <u>pen</u> . . . <u>pen</u>. Draw a circle around the word.

7. Find the picture of the banana. Look at the words in the row. Find the
word <u>got</u> . . . <u>got</u>. Draw a circle around the word.

8. Find the picture of the chair. Look at the words in the row. Find the word
<u>sad</u> . . . <u>sad</u>. Draw a circle around the word.

9. Find the picture of the mitten. Look at the words in the row. Which word
means "more than one"? Circle the word that means "more than one."

10. Find the picture of the umbrella. Look at the words in the row.
Listen: We like to jump. Find the word <u>jump</u> . . . <u>jump</u>. Draw a circle
around the word.

Fox and Stork

1.

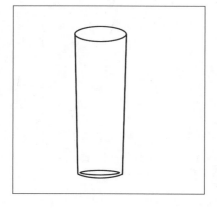 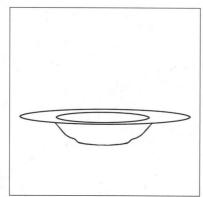 

2.

3.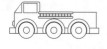

Grade K • Benchmark Advance Weekly and Unit Assessments • © Benchmark Education Company, LLC

4.

5.

Reading Foundational Skills

6.

pan   pen   pin

7.

got   hot   cot

8.

sat   sap   sad

9.

pig   pigs   peg

10.

you   for   jump

STOP!

Reading Skills and Strategy Assessment

Teacher's Name _____ Class _____ Date _____

Directions: Based on classroom observations during Week 1, rate each student's progress in the areas listed below by marking 1, 2, or 3 in the box below each statement. 1=Not Yet; 2=Sometimes; 3=Always. Record any additional notes or comments in the Comments column or at the bottom of the page.

Student Name	Retell Key Details	Identify Cause and Effect	Identify Opinion and Reason	Text Features: Captions, Labels	Vocabulary: Opposites	Use Context Clues	Initial w	High-Frequency Words	Comments/Notes

Foundational Skills Assessment

Teacher's Name _____ Class _____ Date _____

Initial *w*
High-Frequency Words

Directions: To assess or verify the student's reading foundational skills:

1. Read the words in the first row. Ask the student to name the words that begin with *w*.

2. Point to the second row. Ask the student to read the words. Circle each word the student reads correctly.

fin	win	wag	bag
have		are	

Reading Skills and Strategy Assessment

Teacher's Name _____ Class _____ Date _____

Directions: Based on classroom observations during Week 2, rate each student's progress in the areas listed below by marking 1, 2, or 3 in the box below each statement. 1=Not Yet; 2=Sometimes; 3=Always. Record any additional notes or comments in the Comments column or at the bottom of the page.

Student Name	Retell Key Details	Identify Cause and Effect	Author's Reasons	Relate Text and Illustration	Vocabulary: Words Ending in -ed	Use Context Clues / Initial	High-Frequency Words	Comments/Notes

Foundational Skills Assessment

Teacher's Name _____ Class _____ Date _____

Initial *l* / High-Frequency Words

Directions: To assess or verify the student's reading foundational skills:

1. Read the words in the first row. Ask the student to name the words that begin with *l*.

2. Point to the second row. Ask the student to read the words. Circle each word the student reads correctly.

dog	log	rip	lip
He said he has two pets.			

Teacher Administration:
Read the passage aloud as children look at the illustrations.
Then read each question along with the answer choices. Have
children circle the correct answer to each question.

Arbor Day

We celebrate many holidays. On some holidays, we eat
special foods. On some, we get presents or give them to
others. Sometimes we raise the flag. We go to parades. Or we
honor special people.

On Arbor Day, we celebrate trees. This holiday comes on the
last Friday of April each year. That is a good time to plant trees
in many places.

Why do we have a day for trees? Trees do so much for us.
They give us shade in the summer. Many trees protect us. They
block fierce winds all year long. They make the air healthier for
us to breathe. And they are beautiful, too.

Reading Questions

> **Say:** Now I'm going to read some questions. Follow along as
> I read.

1. Find the picture of the apple. Look at the pictures in the row. Why
   is Arbor Day in the spring? Is it because the days are cold . . . it is
   a good time to plant trees . . . or people have free time? Circle the
   picture that shows why Arbor Day is in the spring.

2. Find the picture of the bell. Look at the pictures in the row. Which
   word belongs in the same group as <u>spring</u>? Is it <u>summer</u> . . . <u>flag</u> . . .
   or <u>parade</u>? Circle the answer.

continued

3. Find the picture of the truck. Look at the pictures in the row. Why did the author write this passage: to make you laugh . . . to get you to plant a tree . . . or to teach you about trees? Circle the answer.

4. Find the picture of the pencil. Look at the pictures in the row. Which picture shows trees in summer? Circle the picture.

5. Find the picture of the boot. Look at the pictures in the row. The passage says that many trees protect us. They block fierce winds all year long. Which picture shows what <u>fierce</u> means? Circle the picture.

Reading Foundational Skills Questions

Say: Now look at the next page. I am going to ask some more questions.

6. Find the picture of the spoon. Look at the words in the row. Find the word <u>wet</u> . . . <u>wet</u>. Draw a circle around the word.

7. Find the picture of the banana. Look at the words in the row. Find the word <u>lid</u> . . . <u>lid</u>. Draw a circle around the word.

8. Find the picture of the chair. Look at the words in the row. Find the word <u>jam</u> . . . <u>jam</u>. Draw a circle around the word.

9. Find the picture of the mitten. Look at the words in the row. Listen: This peach is for you. Find the word <u>for</u> . . . <u>for</u>. Draw a circle around the word.

10. Find the picture of the umbrella. Look at the words in the row. Listen: She said hello to me. Find the word <u>said</u> . . . <u>said</u>. Draw a circle around the word.

Arbor Day

1.

2.

3.

4.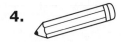

5.

6.

wet   **met**   **net**

7.

bid   **rid**   **lid**

8.

ham   **jam**   **dam**

9.

are   two   for

10.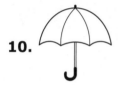

said   see   with

Reading Skills and Strategy Assessment

Teacher's Name _____ Class _____ Date _____

Directions: Based on classroom observations during Week 1, rate each student's progress in the areas listed below by marking 1, 2, or 3 in the box below each statement. 1=Not Yet; 2=Sometimes; 3=Always. Record any additional notes or comments in the Comments column or at the bottom of the page.

Student Name	Retell Key Events	Identify Setting	Relate Text and Illustrations	Vocabulary: Context Clues	Vocabulary: Identify New Meanings	Initial *k*	High-Frequency Words	Comments/Notes

Foundational Skills Assessment

Teacher's Name _____ Class _____ Date _____

Initial *k*
High-Frequency Words

Directions: To assess or verify the student's reading foundational skills:

1. Read the words in the first row. Ask the student to name the words that begin with *k*.

2. Point to the second row. Ask the student to read the words. Circle each word the student reads correctly.

fit	kit	hen	Ken

You can look for me.

Reading Skills and Strategy Assessment

Teacher's Name _____ Class _____ Date _____

Directions: Based on classroom observations during Week 2, rate each student's progress in the areas listed below by marking 1, 2, or 3 in the box below each statement. 1=Not Yet; 2=Sometimes; 3=Always. Record any additional notes or comments in the Comments column or at the bottom of the page.

Student Name	Main Topic and Details	Identify Cause and Effect	Connect Pieces of Information	Vocabulary: Sort Words Into Categories	Vocabulary: Context Clues	Vocabulary: Initial y	High- Frequency Words	Comments/Notes

Foundational Skills Assessment

Teacher's Name _____ Class _____ Date _____

Initial *y*
High-Frequency Words

Directions: To assess or verify the student's reading foundational skills:

1. Read the words in the first row. Ask the student to name the words that begin with *y*.

2. Point to the second row. Ask the student to read the words. Circle each word the student reads correctly.

get	yet	rap	yap

You can come here.

Teacher Administration:
Read the passage aloud as children look at the illustrations.
Then read each question along with the answer choices. Have
children circle the correct answer to each question.

Tara's Surprising Adventure

It had been raining for weeks. Tara put on her boots and her raincoat. She put on her rain hat and got a big umbrella.

Tara wanted to visit her friend Casey. She opened her umbrella, turned it upside down, and climbed in.

But the umbrella boat did not float across the street to Casey's house. It floated down the street and kept going until it reached the river.

"Follow me," said a dolphin. The dolphin swam with Tara all the way to the bay.

"Follow me," said a whale in the bay. The whale swam with Tara to the sea.

"Follow me," said a giant octopus.

Tara floated on the sea for a while. Then the waves began to push her back toward the bay. They pushed her back up the river all the way to Casey's house.

Tara stepped out of the umbrella and rang the bell. "Guess where I've been!" she said when Casey answered the door.

continued ➔

Reading Questions

> **Say:** Now I'm going to read some questions. Follow along as I read.

1. Find the picture of the apple. Look at the pictures in the row. Who swam with Tara in the river? Was it a whale . . . dolphin . . . or octopus? Circle the picture that shows who swam with Tara in the river.

2. Find the picture of the bell. Look at the pictures in the row. What did Tara's boat look like? Circle the picture that shows what her boat looked like.

3. Find the picture of the truck. Look at the pictures in the row. Where does Casey live? Circle the answer.

4. Find the picture of the pencil. Look at the words from the story. Which word goes with <u>river</u> and <u>bay</u>? Is it <u>raincoat</u> . . . <u>bell</u> . . . or <u>sea</u>? Circle the word that goes with <u>river</u> and <u>bay</u>.

5. Find the picture of the boot. Look at the pictures in the row. The story says, "Then the waves began to push her back toward the bay." Which picture shows the meaning of <u>waves</u> in this story? Circle the picture.

Reading Foundational Skills Questions

> **Say:** Now look at the next page. I am going to ask more questions.

6. Find the picture of the spoon. Look at the words in the row. Find the word <u>Kim</u> . . . <u>Kim</u>. Draw a circle around the word.

7. Find the picture of the banana. Look at the words in the row. Find the word <u>yet</u> . . . <u>yet</u>. Draw a circle around the word.

8. Find the picture of the chair. Look at the words in the row. Find the word <u>quit</u> . . . <u>quit</u>. Draw a circle around the word.

9. Find the picture of the mitten. Look at the words in the row. Listen: Here is my chair. Find the word <u>here</u> . . . <u>here</u>. Draw a circle around the word.

10. Find the picture of the umbrella. Look at the words in the row. Listen: We look at the picture. Find the word <u>look</u> . . . <u>look</u>. Draw a circle around the word.

Tara's Surprising Adventure

1.

2.

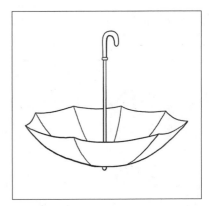  

3.

4.

raincoat	**bell**	**sea**

5.

 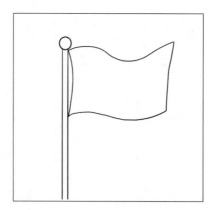 

6.

Tim   **Kim**   **Jim**

7.

vet   **wet**   **yet**

8.

quit   **kit**   **wit**

9.

have   here   are

10.

like   come   look

STOP!

Reading Skills and Strategy Assessment

Teacher's Name _____ Class _____ Date _____

Directions: Based on classroom observations during Week 1, rate each student's progress in the areas listed below by marking 1, 2, or 3 in the box below each statement. 1=Not Yet; 2=Sometimes; 3=Always. Record any additional notes or comments in the Comments column or at the bottom of the page.

Student Name	Retell Story Events	Problem and Solution	Make Inferences About Character	Vocabulary: Sort Words Into Categories	Final x	Initial z	Plurals Using -es	High-Frequency Words	Comments/Notes

Foundational Skills Assessment

Teacher's Name _____ Class _____ Date _____

Final *x*/Initial *z*
High-Frequency Words

Directions: To assess or verify the student's reading foundational skills:

1. Read the words in the first row. Ask the student to name the words that end with *x*.

2. Read the words in the second row. Ask the student to name the words that begin with *z*.

3. Point to the third row. Ask the student to read the words. Circle each word the student reads correctly.

fit	fix	tax	tag
zip	tip	Zeb	Deb
We have two waxes. Look for the foxes.			

Reading Skills and Strategy Assessment

Teacher's Name _____ Class _____ Date _____

Directions: Based on classroom observations during Week 2, rate each student's progress in the areas listed below by marking 1, 2, or 3 in the box below each statement. 1=Not Yet; 2=Sometimes; 3=Always. Record any additional notes or comments in the Comments column or at the bottom of the page.

Student Name	Main Topic and Details	Connect Illustrations and Text	Compare and Contrast	Text Features: Photos, Labels	Vocabulary: Sort Words Into Categories	Vocabulary: Context Clues	Vocabulary: Antonyms	Long a (a_e)	High-Frequency Words	Comments/Notes

Foundational Skills Assessment

Teacher's Name _____ Class _____ Date _____

Long *a (a_e)*
High-Frequency Words

Directions: To assess or verify the student's reading foundational skills, ask the student to read the words in each row. Circle each word the student reads correctly.

same Sam rake gate	
Come here. Look at my cat.	

Teacher Administration:
Read the passage aloud as children look at the illustrations.
Then read each question along with the answer choices. Have
children circle the correct answer to each question.

Needs and Wants

On your birthday, do you ask for things you want? Maybe you want a new bike or a game. But do you really need these things?

Imagine that you are camping in the woods. Would a toy be helpful? Probably not. What you need in the woods is water, some food, and a jacket to keep you warm.

Needs and wants are different. Wants are things that might be fun to have, but you can live without them. Needs are things you must have to live in a healthy way. There are just a few things that you really need to survive. You need food and water. You need clothing to protect you from cold, sun, or bad weather. You need shelter, or a safe place to live. And there is just one more thing everyone needs. We all need love!

Reading Questions

> **Say:** Now I'm going to read some questions. Follow along as
> I read.

1. Find the picture of the apple. Look at the pictures in the row. Which picture shows something a child may want but does not need? Circle the picture of something a child might want.

2. Find the picture of the bell. Look at the pictures in the row. What does everyone need that is not shown in the illustration on page 110? Is it food . . . love . . . or a doll? Circle the answer.

continued ▶

3. Find the picture of the truck. Look at the pictures in the row. Which of these is shown in the picture labeled **Wants**? Circle the answer.

4. Find the picture of the pencil. Look at the pictures in the row. The passage says, "You need shelter." Which picture shows a <u>shelter</u>? Circle the picture.

5. Find the picture of the boot. Look at the words in the row. Which word names something you need: <u>cake</u> . . . <u>bed</u> . . . or <u>rope</u>? Circle the word.

Reading Foundational Skills Questions

Say: Now look at the next page. I am going to ask some more questions.

6. Find the picture of the spoon. Look at the words in the row. Find the word <u>Max</u> . . . <u>Max</u>. Draw a circle around the word.

7. Find the picture of the banana. Look at the words in the row. Find the word <u>zip</u> . . . <u>zip</u>. Draw a circle around the word.

8. Find the picture of the chair. Look at the words in the row. Find the word <u>tape</u> . . . <u>tape</u>. Draw a circle around the word.

9. Find the picture of the mitten. Look at the words in the row. Find the word <u>note</u> . . . <u>note</u>. Draw a circle around the word.

10. Find the picture of the umbrella. Look at the words in the row. Listen: What is your name? Find the word <u>what</u> . . . <u>what</u>. Draw a circle around the word.

STOP!

Needs and Wants

Wants

Needs

1.

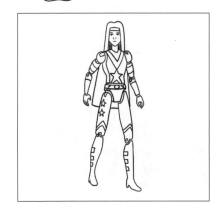  

2.

3.

4.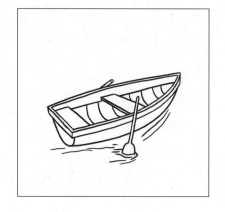

5.

cake   bed   rope

6.

mat   **Max**   **make**

7.

zip   **hip**   **rip**

8.

tap   **top**   **tape**

9.

not   note   Nate

10.

one   with   what

STOP!

Reading Skills and Strategy Assessment

Teacher's Name _____   Class _____   Date _____

Directions: Based on classroom observations during Week 1, rate each student's progress in the areas listed below by marking 1, 2, or 3 in the box below each statement. 1=Not Yet; 2=Sometimes; 3=Always. Record any additional notes or comments in the Comments column or at the bottom of the page.

Student Name	Retell Key Details	Cause and Effect	Text Features: Maps, Captions, Labels	Relate Illustrations and Text	Vocabulary: Opposites	Long *i* (*i_e*)	High-Frequency Words	Comments/Notes

Foundational Skills Assessment

Teacher's Name _____ Class _____ Date _____

Long *i (i_e)*
High-Frequency Words

Directions: To assess or verify the student's reading foundational skills, ask the student to read the words in each row. Circle each word the student reads correctly.

kite	kit	hive	ride
put		want	

Reading Skills and Strategy Assessment

Teacher's Name _____ Class _____ Date _____

Directions: Based on classroom observations during Week 2, rate each student's progress in the areas listed below by marking 1, 2, or 3 in the box below each statement. 1=Not Yet; 2=Sometimes; 3=Always. Record any additional notes or comments in the Comments column or at the bottom of the page.

Student Name	Retell Key Details	Cause and Effect	Text Features: Table of Contents	Connect Illustrations and Text	Vocabulary: Opposites	Vocabulary: Real-Life Connections	Long u (u_e)	High-Frequency Words	Comments/Notes

Foundational Skills Assessment

Teacher's Name _____ Class _____ Date _____

Long *u (u_e)*
High-Frequency Words

Directions: To assess or verify the student's reading foundational skills, ask the student to read the words in each row. Circle each word the student reads correctly.

cube	cub	fume	mule

He saw this rug.

Teacher Administration:
Read the passage aloud as children look at the illustrations.
Then read each question along with the answer choices. Have
children circle the correct answer to each question.

How Your Body Moves

Your body is amazing. You can make it move the way you choose.

Your brain decides which part you want to move and the way you want to move it. Your brain sends a message to that part of your body. The message travels from your brain through your spine. That is the bumpy bone that goes down your back. Then it goes to the part of your body you want to move.

Suppose you want to move your knee or wiggle your toes. The message goes from your brain, down through your backbone, to the muscles in your legs. The muscles help you lift the right bones. The bones are connected to each other with something like rubber bands. This helps the bones move in different ways. All of these parts work together once they get the message.

Reading Questions

Say: Now I'm going to read some questions. Follow along as I read.

1. Find the picture of the apple. Look at the pictures in the row. What part of your body sends a message to make your body move? Circle the picture.

2. Find the picture of the bell. Look at the numbers in the row: 7, 11, 15. Now look at the table of contents (on page 122). On which page of the book can you read more about legs? Circle the number of the page.

continued

3. Find the picture of the truck. Look at the pictures in the row. The passage says your bones are connected with something like—what? Is it screws . . . tape . . . or rubber bands? Circle the answer.

4. Find the picture of the pencil. Look at the words in the row. The passage says the message goes "down through your backbone." Which word means the opposite of <u>down</u>? Circle the word.

5. Find the picture of the boot. Look at the pictures in the row. The passage says the brain sends a message. Sending a message is most like—what? Walking to the store . . . calling someone on the phone . . . or getting dressed? Circle the answer.

Reading Foundational Skills Questions

Say: Now look at the next page. I am going to ask some more questions.

6. Find the picture of the spoon. Look at the words in the row. Find the word <u>line</u> . . . <u>line</u>. Draw a circle around the word.

7. Find the picture of the banana. Look at the words in the row. Find the word <u>mule</u> . . . <u>mule</u>. Draw a circle around the word.

8. Find the picture of the chair. Look at the words in the row. Find the word <u>he</u> . . . <u>he</u>. Draw a circle around the word.

9. Find the picture of the mitten. Look at the words in the row. Listen: Send it to me. Find the word <u>to</u> . . . <u>to</u>. Draw a circle around the word.

10. Find the picture of the umbrella. Look at the words in the row. Listen: We saw a duck. Find the word <u>saw</u> . . . <u>saw</u>. Draw a circle around the word.

How Your Body Moves

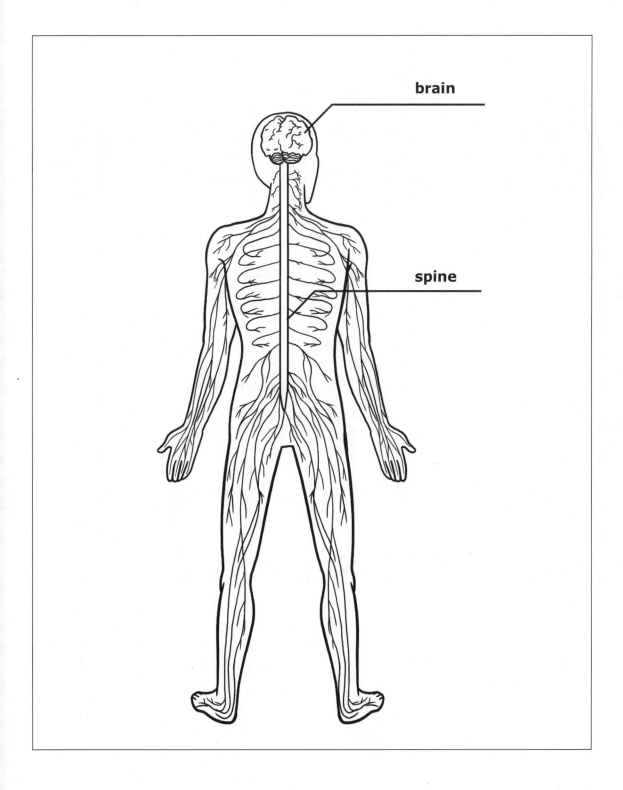

brain

spine

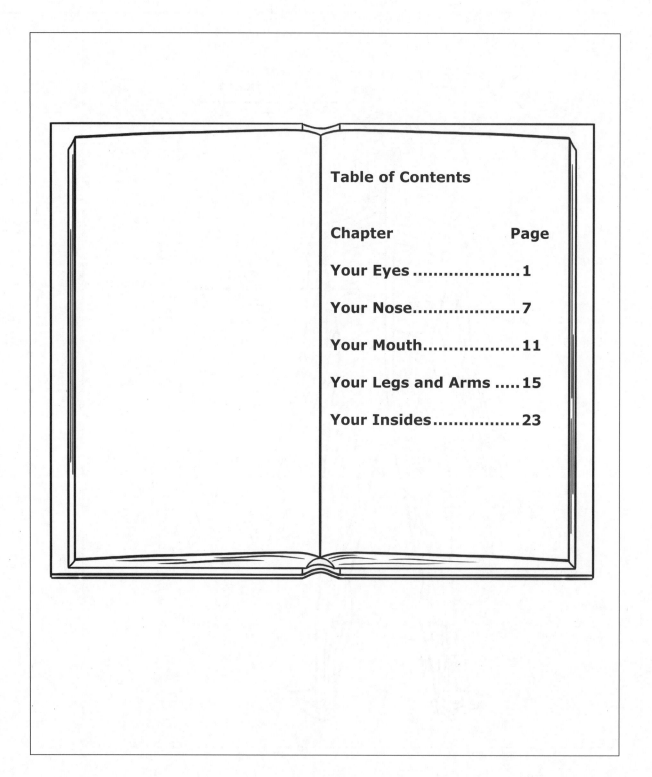

Table of Contents

1.

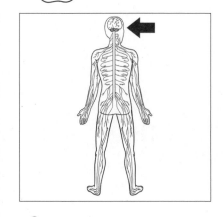 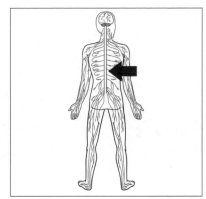 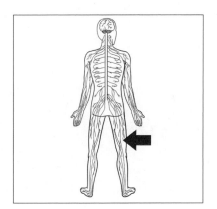

2.

7 **11** **15**

3.

 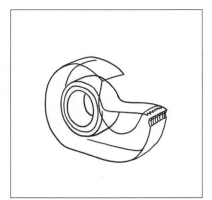 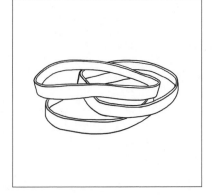

4.

up   **in**   **on**

5.

6.

lone   line   lane

7.

mole   mile   mule

8.

he   hi   ho

9.

go   **to**   **of**

10.

saw   **two**   **she**

STOP!

Unit 1
Answer Keys

Unit 1 Assessment

Question	Answer	Standard Assessed
1.	1st picture (boy reading)	RL.K.7
2.	2nd picture (teacher)	RL.K.3
3.	2nd picture (boy)	RL.K.3
4.	3rd picture (boy looking at plant)	RL.K.1, RL.K.2
5.	2nd picture (girl napping)	RL.K.3
6.	h	RF.K.3a
7.	map	L.K.2d
8.	rim	L.K.2d
9.	sat	L.K.2d
10.	like	RF.K.3c

Unit 1 Scoring

Question	Point Value	Standard Assessed
1.	/	RL.K.7
2.	/	RL.K.3
3.	/	RL.K.3
4.	/	RL.K.1, RL.K.2
5.	/	RL.K.3
6.	/	RF.K.3a
7.	/	L.K.2d
8.	/	L.K.2d
9.	/	L.K.2d
10.	/	RF.K.3c
Total	/	

Unit 2
Answer Keys

Unit 2 Assessment

Question	Answer	Standard Assessed
1.	2nd picture (camel laughing)	RL.K.3
2.	3rd picture (elephant)	RL.K.3
3.	1st picture (lion)	RL.K.1, RL.K.2
4.	1st picture (animals talking)	RL.K.5
5.	3rd picture (hump)	RL.K.3
6.	sat	L.K.2d
7.	tap	L.K.2d
8.	an	L.K.2d
9.	I	RF.K.3c
10.	go	RF.K.3c

Unit 2 Scoring

Question	Point Value	Standard Assessed
1.	/	RL.K.3
2.	/	RL.K.3
3.	/	RL.K.1, RL.K.2
4.	/	RL.K.5
5.	/	RL.K.3
6.	/	L.K.2d
7.	/	L.K.2d
8.	/	L.K.2d
9.	/	RF.K.3c
10.	/	RF.K.3c
Total	/	

Unit 3
Answer Keys

Unit 3 Assessment

Question	Answer	Standard Assessed
1.	1st picture (flies)	RI.K.1, RI.K.2
2.	3rd picture (jaw)	RI.K.4, L.K.4, L.K.6
3.	3rd picture (closed)	RI.K.7
4.	2nd picture (insects)	RI.K.8
5.	2nd picture (leaf)	RI.K.1
6.	sit (medial *i*)	L.K.2d
7.	fan (initial *f*)	L.K.2d
8.	map (final *p*)	L.K.2d
9.	we	RF.K.3c
10.	can	RF.K.3c

Unit 3 Scoring

Question	Point Value	Standard Assessed
1.	/	RI.K.1, RI.K.2
2.	/	RI.K.4, L.K.4, L.K.6
3.	/	RI.K.7
4.	/	RI.K.8
5.	/	RI.K.1
6.	/	L.K.2d
7.	/	L.K.2d
8.	/	L.K.2d
9.	/	RF.K.3c
10.	/	RF.K.3c
Total	/	

Unit 4
Answer Keys

Unit 4 Assessment

Question	Answer	Standard Assessed
1.	3rd picture (three puppies)	RL.K.3
2.	2nd picture (food)	RL.K.4, L.K.5c
3.	1st picture (woman)	RL.K.1, RL.K.2
4.	1st picture (girl with puppy)	RL.K.1
5.	3rd picture (puppies in box)	RL.K.6, RL.K.7
6.	pot	L.K.2d
7.	cap	L.K.2d
8.	hat	L.K.2d
9.	she	RF.K.3c
10.	has	RF.K.3c

Unit 4 Scoring

Question	Point Value	Standard Assessed
1.	/	RL.K.3
2.	/	RL.K.4, L.K.5c
3.	/	RL.K.1, RL.K.2
4.	/	RL.K.1
5.	/	RL.K.6, RL.K.7
6.	/	L.K.2d
7.	/	L.K.2d
8.	/	L.K.2d
9.	/	RF.K.3c
10.	/	RF.K.3c
Total	/	

Unit 5
Answer Keys

Unit 5 Assessment

Question	Answer	Standard Assessed
1.	2nd picture (windmill arm)	RI.K.4, L.K.4a, L.K.6
2.	1st picture (kite)	L.K.5a, L.K.6
3.	3rd picture (direction of wind)	RI.K.5
4.	2nd picture (flour)	RI.K.1, RI.K.2
5.	2nd picture (no electricity)	RI.K.8
6.	bat	L.K.2d
7.	cub	L.K.2d
8.	ran	L.K.2d
9.	big	RF.K.3c
10.	you	RF.K.3c

Unit 5 Scoring

Question	Point Value	Standard Assessed
1.	/	RI.K.4, L.K.4a, L.K.6
2.	/	L.K.5a, L.K.6
3.	/	RI.K.5
4.	/	RI.K.1, RI.K.2
5.	/	RI.K.8
6.	/	L.K.2d
7.	/	L.K.2d
8.	/	L.K.2d
9.	/	RF.K.3c
10.	/	RF.K.3c
Total	/	

Unit 6
Answer Keys

Unit 6 Assessment

Question	Answer	Standard Assessed
1.	2nd picture (wide bowl)	RL.K.4, L.K.5b, L.K.6
2.	2nd picture (wise Stork)	RL.K.3
3.	1st picture (Fox inviting Stork)	RL.K.7
4.	2nd picture (tall, narrow beakers)	RL.K.3
5.	3rd picture (Fox serving Stork)	RL.K.2
6.	pen	L.K.2d
7.	got	L.K.2d
8.	sad	L.K.2d
9.	pigs	L.K.2d
10.	jump	RF.K.3c

Unit 6 Scoring

Question	Point Value	Standard Assessed
1.	/	RL.K.4, L.K.5b, L.K.6
2.	/	RL.K.3
3.	/	RL.K.7
4.	/	RL.K.3
5.	/	RL.K.2
6.	/	L.K.2d
7.	/	L.K.2d
8.	/	L.K.2d
9.	/	L.K.2d
10.	/	RF.K.3c
Total	/	

Unit 7
Answer Keys

Unit 7 Assessment

Question	Answer	Standard Assessed
1.	2nd picture (time to plant)	RI.K.3
2.	1st picture (summer)	L.K.5a
3.	3rd picture (teach about trees)	RI.K.8
4.	1st picture (trees in summer)	RI.K.7
5.	2nd picture (fierce winds)	RI.K.4
6.	wet	L.K.2d
7.	lid	L.K.2d
8.	jam	L.K.2d
9.	for	RF.K.3c
10.	said	RF.K.3c

Unit 7 Scoring

Question	Point Value	Standard Assessed
1.	/	RI.K.3
2.	/	L.K.5a
3.	/	RI.K.8
4.	/	RI.K.7
5.	/	RI.K.4
6.	/	L.K.2d
7.	/	L.K.2d
8.	/	L.K.2d
9.	/	RF.K.3c
10.	/	RF.K.3c
Total	/	

Unit 8
Answer Keys

Unit 8 Assessment

Question	Answer	Standard Assessed
1.	2nd picture (dolphin)	RL.K.1, RL.K.2
2.	3rd picture (umbrella)	RL.K.7
3.	1st picture (house on street)	RL.K.3
4.	sea	L.K.5a
5.	3rd picture (ocean waves)	RL.K.4, L.K.4a
6.	Kim	L.K.2d
7.	yet	L.K.2d
8.	quit	L.K.2d
9.	here	RF.K.3c
10.	look	RF.K.3c

Unit 8 Scoring

Question	Point Value	Standard Assessed
1.	/	RL.K.1, RL.K.2
2.	/	RL.K.7
3.	/	RL.K.3
4.	/	L.K.5a
5.	/	RL.K.4, L.K.4a
6.	/	L.K.2d
7.	/	L.K.2d
8.	/	L.K.2d
9.	/	RF.K.3c
10.	/	RF.K.3c
Total	/	

Unit 9
Answer Keys

Unit 9 Assessment

Question	Answer	Standard Assessed
1.	1st picture (toy)	RI.K.5
2.	2nd picture (heart/love)	RI.K.7
3.	2nd picture (bike)	RI.K.5
4.	3rd picture (hut)	RI.K.4
5.	bed	L.K.5a, L.K.6
6.	Max	L.K.2d
7.	zip	L.K.2d
8.	tape	L.K.2d
9.	note	L.K.2d
10.	what	RF.K.3c

Unit 9 Scoring

Question	Point Value	Standard Assessed
1.	/	RI.K.5
2.	/	RI.K.7
3.	/	RI.K.5
4.	/	RI.K.4
5.	/	L.K.5a, L.K.6
6.	/	L.K.2d
7.	/	L.K.2d
8.	/	L.K.2d
9.	/	L.K.2d
10.	/	RF.K.3c
Total	/	

Unit 10
Answer Keys

Unit 10 Assessment

Question	Answer	Standard Assessed
1.	1st picture (brain)	RI.K.5
2.	15	RI.K.5
3.	3rd picture (rubber bands)	RI.K.1, RI.K.2
4.	up	L.K.5b, L.K.6
5.	2nd picture (calling on phone)	RI.K.4, L.K.5c, L.K.6
6.	line	L.K.2d
7.	mule	L.K.2d
8.	he	L.K.2d
9.	to	RF.K.3c
10.	saw	RF.K.3c

Unit 10 Scoring

Question	Point Value	Standard Assessed
1.	/	RI.K.5
2.	/	RI.K.5
3.	/	RI.K.1, RI.K.2
4.	/	L.K.5b, L.K.6
5.	/	RI.K.4, L.K.5c, L.K.6
6.	/	L.K.2d
7.	/	L.K.2d
8.	/	L.K.2d
9.	/	RF.K.3c
10.	/	RF.K.3c
Total	/	